NAVIGATING CREDENTIALS

A Guide to Developing a Successful Program

CYNTHIA ALLEN, ICE-CCP
JANICE MOORE, ICE-CCP

Contributors:
ASHLEY BARDSLEY, ICE-CCP
ERIN DEIST
LISA SEYFRIED, ICE-CCP

Copyright© 2024 SeaCrest Consulting Company, LLC
All Rights Reserved

ISBN: 979-8-3342-3406-2

Disclaimer: The information in this book is based on our experiences and understanding of accepted best practices for credentialing programs.

While every effort has been made to ensure the accuracy of this information at the time of publication, knowledge, practices, and standards change over time. The information in this book is not meant as legal or technical guidance and is not a substitute for professional advice that is specific to your situation and circumstances. The authors do not represent the views or positions of any outside organizations. Readers should make informed decisions and evaluate recommendations for their specific situations.

TABLE OF CONTENTS

Introduction 1

SECTION 1: EXPLORE

Chapter 1: Is Credentialing the Right Fit? 7
    Define the Program's Purpose 7
    Know the Audience and Industry 9
    Select the Right Credentialing Product 14
    Key Considerations for Exploration 17
    Building to Best Practices 18
    Start with Why 20
    Understand What Comes Next 20

SECTION 2: DEVELOP

Chapter 2: How Do We Develop a Program? 27
    Choose Your Own Adventure 27

Chapter 3: Building an Assessment-Based Certificate (ABC)
    Program 29
    Assembling a Team 29
    Developing the Training Content and Assessment 32
    Develop Policies 35
    Develop a Program Evaluation Mechanism 37
    Publish Program Materials 37

Chapter 4: Building a Professional Certification Program 40
    Assembling a Team 40
    Developing the Certification Program 46
Chapter 5: Policy Development 56
    Policies vs. Procedures... 57
    Standard Operating Procedures.. 57
Chapter 6: Documentation 59
Chapter 7: What About Microcredentials? 61

SECTION 3: MAINTAIN & GROW

Chapter 8: Maintain Momentum 65
    Ongoing Tasks 65
Chapter 9: Continual Improvement 71
    Quality Management 71
    Threat Analysis 73
    Third-Party Accreditation 74
Chapter 10: Planning for Growth 77
References and Resources.. 78
    Accreditation Standards... 78
    Publications 78
    Industry Associations 79
    SeaCrest Toolkits.. 79
Acknowledgments 80
About the Authors 82

Introduction

SEACREST BELIEVES credentialing makes a difference to professionals and the public they serve. Through everything from food-handler training certificates that help prevent foodborne illnesses to ensuring emergency medical responders arrive with the knowledge and skills to safely stabilize a patient, certificates can fill key training gaps, while certifications contribute to public safety in numerous ways. If you have ever eaten in a restaurant, walked safely past a construction site, or received medical care, you have experienced the benefit of personnel credentials.

Every credentialing program, no matter the size, can make a positive impact. We founded SeaCrest in 2006 to help certifying organizations increase quality, improve overall operations, and achieve accreditation by providing expert guidance. While the credentialing field has evolved dramatically since that time, some enduring problems remain.

All too often, organizations dive into a new certification or certificate without either understanding their intended audience, determining if a need exists, or matching the audience's need to the product that fits best. A small, passionate group of volunteers may be convincing advocates for a new program, but that passion rarely translates into a successful program without underlying research, a lot of preliminary groundwork, and a commitment of ongoing resources.

"If you build it, they will come," is more of a joke than a truism in the credentialing community. "Do your homework" serves as a more reliable adage.

If you are planning to create a new certificate or certification program, or if you are just exploring the possibilities, the information presented here will help you navigate the road ahead. While every program is unique—with its own field of knowledge and experts—the process of exploring, developing, building and growing a credential comes with well-established best practices and field-tested principles.

The major milestones for building either an assessment-based certificate or professional certification program are outlined in this book. Here, we will provide a foundational understanding of key concepts so you can make informed decisions about choosing and creating a credentialing program. There is always more to learn, so additional resources are included at the end of this book.

We applied our decades of combined experience working with both successful and struggling programs to create this book. Our lessons learned from building new programs, designing improvements for existing programs, and witnessing the consequences of poor planning are shared here.

NAVIGATING CREDENTIALS

While certainly this is not the only way to create new credentials, the map we outline has proven successful for us and many credentialing programs.

CYNTHIA ALLEN & JANICE MOORE

Section 1: EXPLORE

CYNTHIA ALLEN & JANICE MOORE

Chapter 1

Is Credentialing the Right Fit?

A CREDENTIALING PROGRAM can be a valuable addition to an organization. The right program adds to the portfolio of products and helps meet stakeholder needs. The program's success increases when the sponsoring organization understands the needs of their target audience(s) and commits to carefully planning to build a product to meet them. This is often a step that organizations complete without due consideration or skip entirely.

Certifications, assessment-based certificate programs, and other credentialing products help support the organization's mission and can drive revenue if they are consistent with stakeholder needs.

Define the Program's Purpose

The first step to create a new credentialing product is to define the program's purpose, scope, level, and target audience. All program and exam design decisions should tie back to these foundational elements.

PROGRAMMING NOTE

There are many types of credentials, from academic degrees and government-issued licenses to training certificates and professional certifications.

Certification programs can be entry-level, signify specialty knowledge, or build across a career span. They can be broad in scope or micro-certifications that assess a specific skill, singular or stackable. The same goes for certificate programs that range from a short class to a comprehensive training course with formative and/or summative assessments. They can teach a broad range of skills or focus on a single task. This book focuses on two types of credentials: assessment-based certificate programs and certifications. Within each, there are options for specialties, stackable models, microcredential options, and more.

The Institute for Credentialing Excellence (I.C.E.) defines these program types as follows:

Assessment-Based Certificate Program: A non-degree-granting program that a) provides instruction and training to aid participants in acquiring specific knowledge, skills, and/or competencies associated with intended learning outcomes; b) evaluates participants' achievement of the intended learning outcomes; and c) awards a certificate only to those participants who meet the performance, proficiency, or passing standard on an assessment verifying learning.

Certification Program: The standards, policies, procedures, assessment instruments, and related products and activities through which individuals are publicly identified as having mastered knowledge and skills critical to the successful performance in a profession, occupation, or role.

I.C.E. Terminology Task Force, (2020). *Basic Guide to Credentialing Terminology* (2nd ed.). Institute for Credentialing Excellence.

It is helpful to think of this as the program's mission statement, with the guiding question being, "What should the product or program accomplish for the individual who participates, as well as the organization sponsoring it?"

After identifying a potential credentialing program's *why*, start evaluating the *who, what,* and *how* in more detail. Credentialing programs are less successful when the sponsoring organization does not adequately research the target audience's needs and plan thoughtfully for how to meet them.

Know the Audience and Industry

Identifying and understanding the program's target audience allows organizations to build a profile of the potential certificant or participant, identifying the possible challenges and opportunities they face, and building a product that fits their needs and future goals for professional development.

A target audience profile provides essential information to the sponsoring organization, informing the foundation of the credentialing program. An audience profile can include many data points. A helpful way to organize this data is to include four main categories of information:

1. Demographics
2. Environmental factors
3. Professional development needs
4. Personal needs

A sponsoring organization might already have demographic information on their target audience from previous surveys, such as a Job Analysis study, membership survey, or research projects. If this information is not readily available, however, consider conducting a new survey of the target audience to collect current information. Beyond the value the survey has in gathering information to determine the right type of credentialing product, the results can be used to monitor and identify trends for the target audience and within the industry.

Demographic information might include data points such as age, education level, income level, geographic location, gender, race/ethnicity, practice setting, and/or years of experience. Each sponsoring organization should select the data points that are most relevant to their organization and the potential program.

It is also important for the sponsoring organization to understand the industry. An environmental scan helps organizations understand the current state of the field in which they want to introduce a new credentialing product; what changes may affect practitioners in the field; and what information—training or exams—is needed to help the workforce demonstrate competency and evolve their knowledge, skills, and abilities. Conducting an environmental scan also builds awareness of other organizations serving the industry, products that already exist in the field, and gaps in products or services necessary to the workforce.

To conduct an environmental scan, engage a group of organization staff and subject matter experts (also known as SMEs) to review existing literature, research data, presentations, articles, job data, or other sources of information relevant to the new program. The goal of an environmental scan is to *start* to understand the market and to identify opportunities, challenges, and needs in the industry that could impact the credentialing program or that the program could help to address. It is important for multiple people to be involved in the environmental scan and contribute to the research, to ensure representative and diverse perspectives on the need for and design of the new program.

The third category of building a target audience profile is to identify the professional development needs of the target audience. This can be achieved through online surveys, focus groups, personal interviews, or combinations of these tactics. Gathering this information helps the organization build a product that fills an existing need.

For example, if training in a new area relevant to the field is the highest need, then an assessment-based certificate program that combines training and a summative assessment would likely be a good fit. If the need is to protect the public by assessing minimal competency in a role, then a certification program may be the correct choice.

> ### PROGRAMMING NOTE
>
> While exploring the professional development needs of the target audience, consider the following:
> - What will help the target audience enter the field and then advance in their profession?
> - What does the target audience need to expand their knowledge or fill knowledge gaps?
> - What skills do members of the target audience need?
> - Is there a standard career path in the field with defined milestones?
> - What motivations are there in the field to achieve specific certifications?
> - Do members of the target audience need specific training or certification to get their first job in the field?
> - Do members of the target audience typically need designations after their name to take the next step in their career?

An organization should not only understand the professional development needs of their target audience, but also the target audience's personal needs and how they prefer to engage in professional development activities (e.g., in person, synchronous, asynchronous). This information is centered around how the target audience engages with the organization and its products and services.

While building the target audience profile, the organization can identify common challenges their audience faces in committing to professional development (e.g., cost, time, employer support), trends surrounding in-person and online training, barriers to earning certifications, and ways the organization might overcome those barriers.

A formal Needs Analysis study would help the sponsoring organization gather this information and support the decision-making process. Engaging directly with the target audience through surveys, focus groups, and interviews provides a strong foundation of information. Regardless of the information-gathering tactics used for any of these steps, the sponsoring organization should focus on obtaining information from a varied sample of practitioners that is representative to the program's target audience and key stakeholders.

Organizations might hinder their own progress by limiting their engagement to only a small group of board members, staff, or individuals who already support the potential program or are firm "believers" in the mission and goals of the organization. While these are important perspectives to include in the audience profile and to consider throughout the program-development process, organizations should try to collect a wide variety of perspectives to identify the audience's needs and behavior trends more broadly. The sponsoring organization should intentionally engage with individuals who are outside of the organization, previously involved with the organization, or not fully supportive of the organization, in order to understand a perspective that may not support certification or other new products.

In addition to the target audience profile, there are existing resources and research that the sponsoring organization can use to support the decision-making process and better understand the current market for credentialing programs. Organizations such as the Institute for Credentialing Excellence (I.C.E.) and the Association of Test Publishers (ATP) study and publish information on a variety of topics related to the value of certification and best practices for credentialing programs.

Select the Right Credentialing Product

After ensuring a strong understanding of the needs of the target audience, it is important to define the purpose of the program or product for both the target audience and the sponsoring organization.

While there are several types of credentialing products to consider, this resource focuses on assessment-based certificate programs and professional certification programs. I.C.E. provides a helpful summary of the purposes and attributes of the two program types, laid out in the following page.

Additionally, sponsoring organizations may consider a microcredential model. This model is defined by I.C.E. as, "The formal recognition awarded to an individual who has demonstrated attainment of a narrow (or specific or limited) scope of knowledge, skills, or abilities. The scope of the microcredential can be as granular as a single skill or competency." (*I.C.E. Basic Guide to Credentialing Terminology, 2nd Edition*, 2021)

Assessment-based Certificate Program	Professional or Personnel Certification Program
PURPOSE: Build capacity and recognition of a specialty area of practice or set of skills.	**PURPOSE: Recognize professionals who meet established knowledge, skills, or competencies.**
Provides instruction and training (non-degree granting).	Assesses knowledge, skills, and/or competencies previously acquired.
Goal is for participants to acquire specific knowledge, skills, and/or competencies.	Goal is to validate the participant's competency through a conformity assessment system.
Assessment is used to evaluate mastery of the intended learning outcomes; linked directly to the learning event.	Assessment is best used to assure baseline competencies and to differentiate professionals; independent of a specific learning event.

Assessment-based Certificate Program	Professional or Personnel Certification Program
Assessment content may be narrower in scope.	Assessment content is usually broad in scope.
Awards a certificate to recognize mastery of the specific learning outcomes; it is NOT a certificate of attendance or participation, which is awarded to individuals who have attended or participated in a course or training program but did not have to demonstrate mastery of the intended learning outcomes.	Awards designations to recognize achievement.
To earn accreditation, complies with the *I.C.E. 1100 Standard* and follows the ACAP application procedures.	To earn accreditation, complies with the *NCCA Standards for the Accreditation of Certification Programs* and follows the NCCA application procedures.

I.C.E., (2010). *Defining Features of Quality Certification and Assessment-Based Certificate Programs.* Institute for Credentialing Excellence.

When structuring a credentialing program, consider the needs of the audience and what the organization is aiming to accomplish with the program.

Key Considerations for Exploration

In addition to creating a target audience profile and evaluating the needs of stakeholders, sponsoring organizations should develop an understanding of their market through careful investigation. Market research will explore why a certification program should, or should not, exist.

> ### PROGRAMMING NOTE
>
> **Consider the following questions when selecting the type of credentialing product.**
> - What level (entry, advanced, etc.) is the target audience for the program?
> - Does the target audience need training in the area the program focuses on?
> - Does training already exist? If so, is it offered through the sponsoring organization or another organization?
> - Does the target audience already value or need certification for their role?
> - If there is already a certification in the market, is your organization willing to compete?
> - Is the goal of the credentialing product to *assess* existing knowledge, skill, and ability? Or to *expand* knowledge, skill, and ability in a particular area?
> - What are the sponsoring organization's existing services and strengths?
> - Is the sponsoring organization primarily education or training focused?

A feasibility study is a preliminary exploration of a proposed project to determine its merits and viability. It is a data-driven way to build, develop or expand on the audience profile. This study should evaluate the needs and wants of the potential program's market and the potential role of the program in the market.

A key aspect of the feasibility study is analyzing competition in the market, identifying what needs the program would meet, how it would meet those needs, and if the sponsoring organization is better suited to meet those needs than existing competition. The study should also aim to identify what individuals would want from the program (e.g., training, tests, post-nominal letters), how much people would pay for it, and how it fits into a changing industry or job role.

There are risks to not considering the feasibility of a new program, such as: the program may not meet the needs of the target audience; there may be well-established competition; there may not be enough demand to sustain the program; or the organization might not be able to afford to develop or maintain the program long-term.

Building to Best Practices

When designing a program, it is important to understand that there are generally accepted practices for building a fair, unbiased, quality program. At a minimum, the sponsoring organization should understand and seek to follow these practices to build credibility and minimize legal risk. References and resources related to generally accepted practices are included at the end of this book.

NAVIGATING CREDENTIALS

Beyond these accepted practices, programs can also seek third-party accreditation. Accreditation, as defined by I.C.E., is, "The process by which a credentialing or educational program is evaluated against defined standards by a third party." Accreditation provides a peer-review process that demonstrates a credentialing program meets established standards. Receiving accreditation provides impartial confirmation of the program's quality to credential holders, employers in the industry, and other stakeholders.

It is important to evaluate the competitive environment, stakeholder interests, and any regulatory and/or industry-specific requirements when considering accreditation. While a decision to pursue accreditation can be made at any point, deciding early in the program-design process saves time and resources. Regardless of whether a program chooses to apply for accreditation, following accreditation standards provides a strong foundation and framework for program design and development.

If the sponsoring organization wants to pursue accreditation for the program, the relevant accreditation standards and accrediting body should be selected early in the process to ensure specifics related to the accreditation standards are met as the program is built. In choosing an accreditor—for either a certification or certificate program—consider whether the credential is U.S.-based or international, any regulatory and/or industry-specific requirements, name recognition of the accrediting bodies, specifics of the application process, costs, and the feasibility of meeting the applicable accreditation standards.

Once you've decided to create a credentialing program, the next step is deciding what type of credential to develop. The information collected in the exploration stage outlined in Section 1 helps inform that decision.

Start with Why

Understanding the program's purpose and target audience, the need it will fill, and what it should measure will provide you with a starting point to inform the program type and scope. The credential should support the needs identified in the exploration stage.

If the target audience needs training, an assessment-based certificate program (ABC) may be the best fit. ABCs provide need-based training and evaluate participants against clearly defined learning objectives. Participants who successfully complete the course and assessment(s) earn a certificate. ABCs are well suited when the target audience needs to expand their skills or fill a training gap.

If the need centers on testing whether the target audience has sufficient knowledge, skills, and/or abilities (KSAs), a certification program is likely appropriate. Professional certification, or personnel certification, tests an individual against a pre-determined standard. Certifications are a good match when the target audience needs to demonstrate they have the KSAs necessary for a specific job, role or task.

Understand What Comes Next

Before committing to an assessment-based certificate program or a certification program, it helps to understand the process involved in developing, and maintaining, each type of program. The table below indicates some key milestones. This is not an all-inclusive list.

Launch

Assessment-Based Certificate

- Develop core policies (e.g., prerequisites)
- Conduct needs analysis
- Develop training content and assessment
- Deliver the course
- Issue certificates

Define purpose, need, scope, audience
Form decision-making, governing body
Assign resources (e.g., staff, consultants, vendors, technology)
Recruit and select SMEs
Publish key program information
Accept applications

- Develop core policies (e.g., eligibility, recertification, code of conduct)
- Conduct job task/practice analysis
- Develop examination
- Deliver the test
- Issue credentials

Certification

Maintenance

Assessment-Based Certificate

- Evaluate the course
- Conduct ongoing training content evaluation

Adjust and improve

- Evaluate test performance
- Conduct ongoing item development and exam updates
- Conduct a job task/practice analysis (typically every 5-7 years)

Certification

Among the many milestones, perhaps the most time and resource intensive are training content development for an assessment-based certificate program and exam development for a certification program. Key steps involved in each are outlined on the next page.

Assessment-Based Certificate Content Development	Certification Exam Development
Needs Analysis	
Research/Job Task Analysis	Job Task Analysis
Design Document	Exam Specifications
Content Development	Item Development
Assessment Development	Exam Form Development
	Pilot/Beta Testing
Cut Score for Assessment	Cut Score Study
Select Education and Assessment Delivery Methods	Select Exam Delivery Methods
Evaluate Outcomes	Item and Test Analysis
Ongoing Maintenance	Ongoing Maintenance

Successful programs result from an informed decision-making process. Understanding who the audience is, their current needs, and emerging trends help organizations launch a valuable program for stakeholders. Equally helpful is to understand the type of credentialing products available and the role they serve to the audience.

CYNTHIA ALLEN & JANICE MOORE

NAVIGATING CREDENTIALS

Section 2:
DEVELOP

CYNTHIA ALLEN & JANICE MOORE

Chapter 2

How Do We Develop a Program?

ONCE YOU CHOOSE your destination, whether certification or certificate, the next step includes planning how to get there. After finishing the process outlined in Section 1, you should understand the options, the need for a credential, and the type of credentialing product that fits your target audience and purpose. The next step focuses on developing your selected credential.

You are at the starting point, with a clear direction in mind and ready to choose either an ABC program or certification program. Keep in mind that your program can, and should, evolve as the needs of your audience the market change. There may be a "right" program fit now, and additional programs may be added later. Developing a credential is a continual process of evaluation and adaptation.

Choose Your Own Adventure

Each type of credential serves a specific purpose for the target audience and sponsoring organization. While there is some overlap in the development processes, we will discuss each program type separately so readers can focus on the most relevant information for the program type they have selected. Areas common to both ABC programs and certifications are discussed in Chapter 5: Policy Development and Chapter 6: Documentation.

Chapter 3: Building an Assessment-Based Certificate Program outlines the key steps in the development of an ABC program. Chapter 4: Building a Professional Certification Program, addresses the key milestones for certification program development.

Chapter 7: What About Microcredentials, addresses key considerations for organizations intending to launch a microcredential program.

Chapter 3

Building an Assessment-Based Certificate (ABC) Program

Assembling a Team

Developing an ABC program relies on a team of professionals and subject matter experts (SMEs) to manage project tasks and schedules, develop training content, guide assessment development, and more.

Subject Matter Experts (SMEs)

Gathering a team of subject matter experts (SMEs) who represent the diversity of your target audience and the program stakeholders provides a great place to start developing your new ABC program. SMEs play a variety of roles in the development process. An initial group of SMEs serves as an oversight or advisory group to inform the ABC program-development process and set essential program policies. This group can go by many names and take many forms, but for our purposes, we will refer to this group as the Steering Committee.

While the SMEs on the Steering Committee provide leadership and policy-level input for the program, additional SMEs develop the course and exam content. All SME groups should be diverse and representative of the program's target audience. SMEs with varied perspectives, backgrounds, and experience levels bring relevancy and value to the program and its intended audience. The SMEs may also serve as course instructors, if applicable, based on how the course is offered.

Project Manager

A strong Project Manager coordinates and supports the work of the SMEs and other personnel, including vendors or consultants, according to the defined budget and timeline. The sponsoring organization may assign this role to internal staff or outsource it to a consultant. Regardless of who fills the role, a Project Manager with clearly defined roles and responsibilities plays an essential part in the program's success.

Other Personnel

Just as SMEs provide valuable knowledge in the program subject area, there is value in recruiting expertise in ABC program development. Engaging outside consultants or vendors with specific experience in developing ABC programs helps complete the development team. These professionals bring valuable knowledge of best practices that can streamline the process and help you avoid making common—and costly—mistakes.

Consider utilizing the following experts, as needed, on the development team.

Instructional Designer: These professionals bring know-how in applying instructional design practices to assess learner needs, identify training content, design engaging learning activities, and facilitate SME course content development. Instructional Designers contribute their understanding of how people learn and the most effective methods and materials to help your program meet its defined objectives.

Psychometrician: These professionals are proficient in developing assessments, helping to ensure that the summative assessment for the ABC program measures what it is intended to measure. For ABC programs, Psychometricians can design and facilitate the Job Analysis study (as needed), train SMEs to write exam questions, set the passing point for the exam, and evaluate the performance of the exam as a whole, as well as evaluate performance of the individual exam questions.

Attorney: Legal experts help develop agreements with instructors, other SMEs, and participants to protect your organization's intellectual property. They should also be engaged to establish the entity that houses the program, if one does not already exist.

Credentialing and/or Accreditation Consultants: Experienced consultants provide project management assistance for program design, assist in developing policies, and guide the program in meeting best practices and/or third-party accreditation requirements.

Outsourced personnel provide tremendous value and efficiency. However, the sponsoring organization that implements the ABC program should maintain ultimate authority and responsibility for essential program decisions including:

- ✓ Defining the program's purpose and scope.
- ✓ Establishing the eligibility requirements (if any).
- ✓ Establishing the requirements for earning the certificate (e.g., completing training, passing the assessment).
- ✓ Issuing the certificate.

Developing the Training Content and Assessment

The steps below represent a high-level summary of ABC program development. As discussed in the Introduction, a variety of organizations serving the credentialing community offer detailed guidance. Refer to the References and Resources section at the end of this book for additional information.

Conduct a Needs Analysis

Creating an ABC program begins with a Needs Analysis, a formal study of the target audience, to understand specific training needs and learning preferences. The results guide all subsequent program design decisions.

Conducting a Needs Analysis is not a solo endeavor. Soliciting input from a diverse group of SMEs and stakeholders helps ensure the organization considers a variety of perspectives and that the resulting course represents the needs of the larger target audience.

Develop Training Content

Make sure you document a clear connection between the results of the Needs Analysis and each course component, including the learning outcomes, training content, and the method(s) for delivery. Design and develop the course intentionally, following an accepted instructional design method (e.g., ADDIE or other common models).

While tempting, and sometimes faster, to rely on the expertise of one or two well-established experts, you should engage plenty of SMEs to develop training content under the guidance of an Instructional Designer. Select SMEs carefully, based on pre-determined qualifications, to ensure they represent the program's target audience and key stakeholders.

How the program will be delivered is a key part of the design process. Make these decisions early in the process so that the course can be designed to best fit the planned delivery methods. Use the data collected during the Needs Analysis to inform decisions about whether the program will be in-person or online, live or asynchronous, etc.

For example, if instructors will be delivering the training to participants, you should account for training and evaluating instructors as you develop the program.

Develop the Assessment

The ABC program exists to determine if the participants attained the intended learning outcomes. A summative assessment, an exam taken at the completion of the training, is a common method to evaluate mastery of the intended learning outcomes. Formative assessments, exams that occur throughout the training to measure progress toward learning objectives, may also be included. Exams and question (or item) types take many forms, from multiple-choice items, essays, and short answer to assembling a portfolio as a demonstration of mastery.

Document your methodology in order to ensure the assessment, in whatever form it takes, serves the intended purpose of the program. This includes confirming that the learning outcomes link to the assessment items. Include a formal Job Analysis study for programs categorized as "high stakes," meaning they are associated with substantial potential for adverse consequences for the public, clients, patients, or other stakeholders.

After developing the assessment, you should also document the methodology and process to determine the summative-assessment passing score, along with how you will monitor the assessment to ensure it is performing as intended.

Deliver the Program

Participants' preferences for program delivery are informed by the Needs Analysis. The instructional portion of the ABC program can be provided in-person with an instructor, remotely, through self-led progress through instructional materials, or some mix of these options. For example, in a synchronous learning environment, the participants gather and interact in real time. Participants in an asynchronous learning environment access materials at their own pace and have varying levels of interaction with other participants, or may have no interaction at all. Depending on the selected delivery method, the program may include an instructor training process and the creation of standardized course materials.

Technology is also a key program-delivery element. Unless the program is only offered in person, you will most likely invest in a learning management system (LMS) to deliver the training. An LMS delivers summative and formative assessments and tracks participants' progress through the training. Finally, consider a secure candidate management system (CMS) to track participants' contact information and certificate completion status in order to manage communications.

Develop Policies

Policies serve a foundational purpose in the development of any ABC program. They support fairness and consistent decision making. Policies are established during the development period and then reviewed periodically as the program matures, to ensure they remain current.

While policies may vary based on the organization, the industry the program serves, and the stakes of the program (high or low stakes), a list of <u>core</u> policies for ABC programs is as follows:

- ✓ Confidentiality
- ✓ Conflict of interest
- ✓ Personnel qualifications (staff, volunteer leaders, committees, instructors, subject matter experts, etc.)
- ✓ Vendor management and oversight
- ✓ Policy review
- ✓ Nondiscrimination and fairness
- ✓ Program evaluation
- ✓ Document management and records retention
- ✓ Security
- ✓ Quality management
- ✓ Eligibility (prerequisites) and application processing
- ✓ Complaints, appeals, and disciplinary policy
- ✓ ADA accommodations
- ✓ Subject matter experts
- ✓ Instructors
- ✓ Training content development and maintenance
- ✓ Assessment development and maintenance
- ✓ Training and assessment delivery

Develop a Program Evaluation Mechanism

Create a mechanism for evaluating the training content and effectiveness of the summative assessment during the program development process. Even though the evaluation occurs after the launch of the program, planning how you will conduct evaluations and use evaluation data is essential.

Periodic program evaluation contributes to the ongoing relevancy and value of the program to the target audience and other stakeholders. A periodic and comprehensive review process monitors all elements of the program, including the performance of instructors, the appropriateness of training content, assessment performance, etc. The review mechanism should include feedback from participants, instructors (if applicable), and SMEs.

Publish Program Materials

When publishing information about the program, include information for participants and the general public regarding the purpose and objectives of the program, as well as the requirements to complete the program and the information covered.

As the program sponsor, you should make the following information publicly available:

- ✓ Target audience
- ✓ Purpose and scope
- ✓ How to apply
- ✓ Fees
- ✓ Description of the training and learning outcomes

- ✓ Description of the assessment
- ✓ Description of the SMEs involved in the development of the training
- ✓ Description of the qualifications to serve as an instructor
- ✓ Prerequisites, if applicable
- ✓ Expiration date or renewal requirements, if applicable
- ✓ Program policies, including policies related to filing complaints and appeals of decisions
- ✓ Disciplinary policies (e.g., misrepresentation, cheating, misuse of certificate, policy violations)
- ✓ ADA accommodations
- ✓ Certificates

Participants receive a certificate after completing the required training and passing the summative assessment. Whether you issue a paper certificate, wallet card, or digital badge, the certificate should clearly state the certificant's name, the organization providing the certificate, the program title, the certificate issue date, and the expiration date (if applicable).

There are different schools of thought on offering a designation—for example, letters or acronym after the individual's name—to someone who completes an ABC program. There is general agreement that certificate-program participants do not use letters after their name, because the certificate indicates attainment only of the intended learning outcomes at a point of time. A certification indicates confirmation of knowledge, skills, and/or abilities along with a recertification or renewal mechanism that provides a different level of assurance to the public.

Instead of an acronym after their name, participants who complete an ABC program communicate that they hold a certificate in XYZ or have completed XYZ certificate course. They should not claim to be XYZ-certified or list XYZ after their name.

Chapter 4

Building a Professional Certification Program

Assembling a Team

Successful professional certification program development depends on the contributions of a team of professionals who each bring a unique perspective to the project. The development team includes organizational staff, volunteer leaders, SMEs, psychometricians, test developers, vendors responsible for exam delivery, attorneys, and consultants.

Steering Committee & Certification Governing Body

A group of professionals who represent the certification program target audience should constitute the body responsible for making certification decisions. Start by assembling an initial group of decision-makers, such as a Steering Committee, to guide initial program development. This group informs establishing the requirements for the permanent Certification Governing Body (CGB) and may transition into the initial CGB.

NAVIGATING CREDENTIALS

The Steering Committee and CGB roles and responsibilities include those listed below. These leaders monitor interpretations and decisions with close attention to consistency, fairness, and precedent.

- Developing the standards for initial certification by incorporating input from key stakeholders and based on the results of a required Job Analysis study designed and facilitated by a psychometrician.
- Establishing, reviewing, and adhering to certification program policies.
- Granting initial and ongoing certification to individuals who meet established eligibility and recertification requirements.
- Overseeing the development, maintenance, administration, and scoring of the certification examination.
- Verifying certification status to stakeholders.
- Establishing a process to receive and investigate complaints related to certificants, including a process for sanctions, suspensions, revocation, and appeals.
- Engaging in succession planning to ensure a healthy pipeline of future volunteer leaders, subject matter experts for test development activities, and committee members.
- Providing relevant, accurate, and timely communications and appropriate levels of customer service.

- Supporting quality management by evaluating and monitoring the application review processes, volunteer and staff workload, customer service, test development and administration process, and other factors.
- Conducting all activities free from conflicts of interest and/or undue influence from internal or external individuals, groups, or entities.
- Upholding high ethical standards.

These functions are supported by, and in many cases delegated to, support staff. However, the CGB maintains the authority for the decision-making related to key program and policy decisions.

Staff

The CGB makes program and policy decisions with the option to delegate activities to staff who are responsible for consistent implementation of those decisions. Staff play an essential role in guiding program development in alignment with the budget, timelines, and best practices. You can supplement the staff team with outside consultants who bring expertise and experience in the development of professional certification programs.

Staff with access to confidential exam information cannot also take responsibility for the development or delivery of training resources designed to prepare candidates to take the exam. Maintaining separation between certification program activities and the educational and/or training activities that prepare candidates for the certification exam, such as study guides, review courses, and exam preparation courses, is key to preserving the impartiality of the certification process, complying with best practices, and meeting third-party accreditation requirements for certification programs.

Subject Matter Experts (SMEs)

The importance of SMEs cannot be overstated. Qualified SMEs must participate in the development of the certification exam. SMEs participating in exam-development activities represent the population being certified and should reflect the diversity of that population. This ensures that a variety of perspectives and experiences are built into the process.

To accomplish this, first define the common demographics of the intended certificant population. This includes defining the data points most relevant to the industry and population being certified. Commonly considered demographics include educational background, years of experience, years certified, geographic location, gender, race and ethnicity, practice setting, etc.

Once the population's demographics are understood, actively recruit SMEs who represent that demographic profile. The extra effort needed to accomplish recruiting a wide array of SMEs pays off in the quality and relevance of the exam content.

Outline the SME panel structure in the program's policies. Panels can be organized as ad-hoc committees or standing committees, but either way, you should include term limits or other mechanisms to prevent the same SMEs from serving in multiple roles and/or over multiple years. Consider the options carefully and adopt a structure that best supports the goal of a diverse and representative pool of SMEs and protects the process from the undue influence of any individual(s) or group.

Similar to staff, SMEs with access to confidential exam information cannot participate in developing or delivering resources designed to prepare candidates for the certification exam. This prevents "teaching to the test" and avoids conflicts of interest. Allowing SMEs to participate in training or exam-preparation activities is analogous to insider trading. It would be unfair for an SME to provide certification candidates with information when they obtained that information using non-public, confidential information about the exam.

A good guideline is that training and exam preparation products should be developed with publicly available information, such as the weighted exam content outline.

Other Personnel

SMEs provide required knowledge in the certification program subject area. Experts with specific knowledge related to building certification programs and exams are needed to complete the development team.

These professionals support program development, know how to apply best practices, and understand third-party accreditation standards. They help the organization avoid costly mistakes and streamline the development process. These experts may be consultants or vendors, or they may serve as in-house staff depending on the organization developing the program.

No certification exam should be developed without involving an experienced psychometrician from the beginning stages. According to the *I.C.E. Basic Guide to Credentialing Terminology* (*2nd edition*), a psychometrician is, "An individual who practices the science of educational and psychological measurement (i.e., testing). Psychometricians evaluate the validity, reliability, and fairness of an examination, among other tasks."

Psychometricians design, facilitate, and/or oversee the Job Analysis study, test-form development, standard-setting process (e.g., setting the passing score on the exam), and they conduct item and test analysis. Additional test developers can supplement the exam development team and bring experience in training SMEs to develop exam items.

Accreditation consultants play a key role in the team, particularly if third-party accreditation is a goal. Their role includes helping the development team and volunteer leaders understand third-party accreditation requirements, including how they are interpreted and applied. Accreditation consultants also bring experience around designing governance and organization structure, policy and procedure development, and a broad knowledge of best practices.

Finally, consult an attorney for assistance in determining the appropriate structure of the CGB, ensuring practices are in place to protect confidential information and the organization's intellectual property.

Technology Support

You will be building processes for application review, applicant, candidate and certificant management; item and exam development; issuing credentials, etc. So do consider how those processes can be automated and/or supported with technology. In some cases, vendor contracts include technology products, such as an exam-development vendor who provides access to a secure item development platform.

Developing the Certification Program

Launching a new professional certification program is a complex endeavor requiring tasks across several categories, including the structure and governance of the organization administering the program, establishing policies and procedures to promote fairness and standardization, publishing program information to the public, developing an exam, and administering the exam to candidates. This section outlines a high-level summary of the major milestones associated with developing a certification program. Refer to the References and Resources section at the end of this book for additional information.

Establish the Governance and Structure

One of your first tasks in creating a new program is establishing the governing body responsible for policy and program decisions and creating the structure of the organization administering the program. As noted earlier, start by assembling an initial group of decision-makers, such as a Steering Committee, to guide initial program development. This group helps establish the requirements for the governing body and may transition into the permanent CGB.

There are several options for structuring a certifying organization. Certifications are commonly administered by non-profit organizations; however, for-profit entities also provide a viable option. The structure selected should ensure the CGB can make decisions in the best interest of the certification program, in order to preserve the credibility of the certification and the integrity of the process. The CGB's structure should protect impartial decision making.

Two of the most common non-profit structures for certifying bodies are discussed below. While not the only two possibilities, both occur frequently and work well in most situations.

Stand-Alone Certifying Entity: In the stand-alone model, the CGB is a separately incorporated legal entity, typically with non-profit 501(c)6 tax status. The organization's primary purpose is providing certification, and it does not have members. Certificants, and ultimately the public they serve, are the primary audience.

The organization may develop education and/or training products to support candidates seeking certification. If so, mechanisms are in place to protect confidential exam content and the integrity of the certification process. This structure is illustrated in the following figure, on the next page.

Stand-Alone Certifying Entity

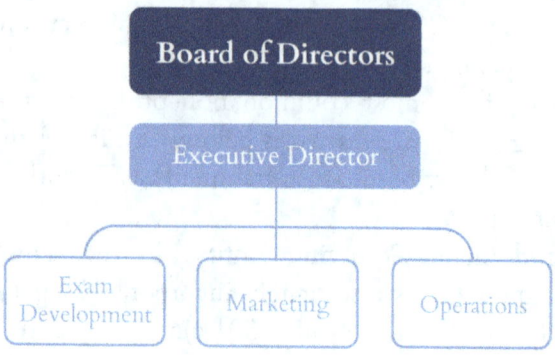

Housed within a Parent Organization: Another common model for non-profit entities includes housing the CGB within a parent organization, such as a professional society or membership association. The CGB in this model functions independently with little influence from the leadership of the parent organization.

The association may have membership services, provide training and/or education, conduct research, etc., while the certification program is operated under the auspices of the independent CGB within the association. The CGB has authority and autonomy to make essential certification decisions.

The figure below illustrates this structure.

Certifying Entity within a Parent Organization

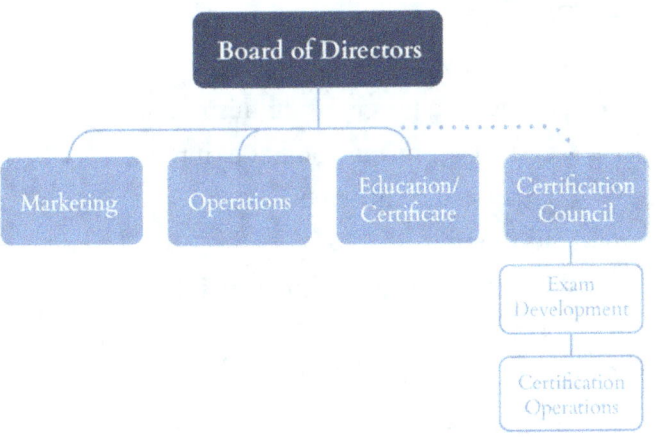

Develop Policy

Established policies enable standardized approaches and promote fairness and consistency for candidates and certificants. They guide decision making and support the credibility of the organization and the certification granted. Policies are established during the development period and then reviewed periodically as the program matures to ensure they remain current.

Policies may vary based on the organization and the industry the program serves. Here is a list of recommended certification program policies:

- ✓ Governance
- ✓ Authority, roles and responsibilities of the governing body
- ✓ Composition and selection process
- ✓ CGB onboarding and orientation
- ✓ Impartiality
- ✓ Certification program administration
- ✓ Confidentiality and conflict of interest
- ✓ Operational management
- ✓ Staff training
- ✓ Vendor management and oversight
- ✓ Policy review
- ✓ Candidate feedback
- ✓ Quality management
- ✓ Security
- ✓ Verification of certification
- ✓ Nondiscrimination and fairness
- ✓ Eligibility requirements and application processing
- ✓ Complaints, disciplinary process, appeals
- ✓ Recertification requirements and application processing
- ✓ ADA accommodations
- ✓ Examination
- ✓ Subject Matter Expert qualifications and selection
- ✓ Examination development and maintenance
- ✓ Examination administration

Policy decisions fall under the authority of the CGB. The CGB may delegate policy implementation and day-to-day management to staff, other SMEs or volunteers, or vendors. Policies are updated or adjusted as the program matures through a required, periodic review process.

Develop the Certification Exam

Well-established best practices exist to guide exam development. Keep in mind that exam development is not a one-time event. Rather, exams require an ongoing cycle of development and review to ensure the content stays current and relevant and the exam performs as intended. The exam development process requires psychometric expertise, SME involvement, and a variety of tasks that may be adjusted based on the type of exam used.

The following list describes a few of the major exam-development milestones. There are many excellent exam-development resources; see the References and Resources section at the end of this book for more information.

Job Analysis Study: Also known as a Job Task Analysis, Role Delineation Study, or Practice Analysis, the Job Analysis is any of several methods used singly or in combination to identify the performance domains and associated tasks, knowledge, and/or skills relating to the purpose of the credential. The Job Analysis provides the foundation for examination validation.

The outcome includes an exam content outline that defines the domains, knowledge, and task statements on the exam, assigns the corresponding content-area weights, and informs exam-design decisions. Job Analysis studies are typically conducted every five years.

Item Development: Following approval of the exam content outline, SMEs develop the items (or questions) on the exam. Items require several levels of review and quality control before appearing on an exam. Item writing usually occurs annually to build a sufficient pool of items.

Exam Assembly: After a sufficient bank of items is developed, reviewed, and approved for use, an exam form(s) is assembled. The exam form also goes through additional review prior to use. Most programs plan for multiple versions, or forms, of the exam to ensure failing candidates retest on a different test form than their initial attempt. As new forms are developed, typically annually, old forms are retired.

Exam Delivery: New certification programs usually plan a beta, or pilot, test of the exam to gather data before setting the passing score. All exam administrations must be secure and standardized.

Standard Setting: The initial testing results inform the standard-setting (or cut-score) process to determine the exam's passing score. Once a passing point is determined, scoring is completed, and candidates receive their score reports.

Test and Item Analysis: The program's psychometrician monitors the performance of exams and items on an ongoing basis. This analysis process identifies poorly performing items, flags potential security concerns, and monitors the overall health of the exam.

PROGRAMMING NOTE

Certification programs should make the following information publicly available through a certification handbook and/or website:

- Description of the certification and the value of certification
- Eligibility requirements
- How to apply: application process, fees, how to schedule an exam
- Information about the exam: how the exam is developed, description of the exam (e.g., number of items, type(s) of items, length of time, exam content outline, reference list)
- Information about taking the exam: what to expect on exam day, how to request special accommodations, policies on exam security and cheating, how exam results are provided, and a retesting policy for candidates that fail the exam
- Maintenance of certification: recertification, reinstatement
- Code of conduct/ethics: requirements, complaints process, and disciplinary policies (including appeals)
- Other policies: how certification status is verified and what information is publicly available, confidentiality, nondiscrimination statement, use of the credential/certification mark
- Application forms: for initial certification and recertification, request for accommodations form

Publish Program Information

Candidate fairness and standardization are foundational elements of a legally defensible certification program. To promote these concepts, organizations publish information about the program and requirements. Easily accessible information related to the target audience, scope, and purpose of the program should be available to stakeholders. This supports transparency and helps the public understand what the certification means.

Additionally, candidates for certification need sufficient information to make an informed decision about seeking the certification, including how to earn and maintain certification and under what conditions the organization can revoke certification.

Administer the Exam

Understanding exam delivery and making an exam-delivery plan is part of the exam design process. Programs have options when considering how the certification exam will be administered. Most exams are delivered by computer-based testing, either in person at testing centers or via live, remote proctoring. While not as common, some programs still use paper-and-pencil testing. Regardless of the delivery method, the principles of fairness, security, and standardization should guide exam administration decisions.

The investment of time and effort to develop a certification exam is significant. At every step of the way, take care to protect that investment by keeping exam content secure. Factor in the need to protect confidential exam content and mitigate opportunities for cheating.

NAVIGATING CREDENTIALS

Candidates also invest their time, effort, and financial resources in preparing for the exam. They should never be disadvantaged based on inconsistencies in exam delivery. A candidate should only fail an exam because they do not have the required knowledge, skills, or abilities as defined by the Job Analysis and not because of the testing environment or other irrelevant factors.

Chapter 5
Policy Development

POLICIES ARE A VALUABLE tool for credentialing programs. They establish the rules that govern participation in the program and create a standardized approach to common situations that credentialing programs encounter. More importantly, policies support consistent and fair decision making.

At some point, all programs receive requests to make an exception to a rule. For example, a candidate who asks for an extension to a deadline, contests their score results, or asks to bypass an eligibility requirement. In each of these situations, it is important to follow a consistent set of rules for legal reasons and to ease confusion among staff or volunteers about how to handle it. Avoiding arbitrary decision making helps the organization reduce potential risk and legal liability.

As the program evolves and grows, it is critical that the established, approved program policies continue to drive decisions. Program policies are intended to be living and dynamic documents, however. Conducting periodic policy review (e.g., annually) with volunteer leaders and staff ensures that policies and program decisions are applied consistently, implemented fairly, and remain current with the needs of the organization and its stakeholders.

Policies vs. Procedures

It is important to make the distinction between a policy, a procedure, and a work instruction.

Work instructions are a set of step-by-step instructions to explain how to complete a task. For example, how to update an individual's address in the database. Work instructions are typically documented for key tasks.

A **procedure** is the steps taken to complete a process. The steps taken to process a program application, or the steps for conducting an item-writing workshop, for example.

A **policy** is the description of what the program is required to do. For example, a policy prohibiting anyone from earning a certificate unless they've completed the course and passed the summative assessment or a policy defining the qualifications for course instructors are policies related to an ABC program. Similarly, a certification program's policy might prohibit an individual from earning the certification without meeting all the established eligibility requirements and passing the certification exam.

Standard Operating Procedures

One method for ensuring consistent implementation of policies is to maintain standard operating procedures (SOPs). SOPs direct staff and volunteers in the execution of their duties and help maintain continuity in instances of turnover.

Think of SOPs as a tool to answer the *how* (and sometimes the *where* and *when*) to the *what* and *why* described in policies. For example, if the staff member assigned to application processing left their position today, how would a remaining/new staff member know what steps to take to process an application?

PROGRAMMING NOTE

Many factors affect the standard operating procedures that your program develops, including policy requirements, technology, etc. Below is a list of common SOPs for credentialing programs:

- Database management
- Application processing
- Quality audit procedures
- Accommodations-request processing
- Exam scheduling
- Issuing candidate score reports and certificates/badges
- Recruiting SMEs
- Planning exam/assessment development meetings
- Proctor training
- Security procedures
- Governing body orientation
- Monitoring exam results
- Verifying candidate/participant status
- Appeals processing
- Monitoring for misuse of the credential

Chapter 6
Documentation

DOCUMENTATION OF EACH step of the program-development process is not only helpful, but is often required. This is especially important as staff and volunteers change over time. A summary report addressing the who, what, when, why, and how of each activity provides a valuable record and serves as a reference point for the ongoing maintenance of the program. It also serves as institutional knowledge on the rationale for program-design decisions.

A summary report should include the following information:

➢ Documentation of the SMEs, staff, vendors, and consultants involved in the activity with the corresponding qualifications.
➢ Description of how the participants were trained to complete the activity.
➢ Documentation of the date of the activity.
➢ Summary of the purpose of the activity and the steps the participants completed.

> Discussion of the methodology used, why the methodology was selected, and how it was applied.
> Summary of the results or outcomes.

> ### PROGRAMMING NOTE
>
> As the old saying goes, "If it's not documented, it didn't happen."
>
> Documenting policies, rationales, major milestones, program-design decisions, participant qualifications, etc. is key to meeting best practices.
>
> Keep records from the outset and throughout program development. This evidence is necessary for accreditation and will prevent repeating discussions and potentially costly steps along the way.

Chapter 7
What About Microcredentials?

THE INSTITUTE FOR CREDENTIALING Excellence (I.C.E.) defines a microcredential as, "the formal recognition awarded to an individual who has demonstrated attainment of a narrow (or specific or limited) scope of knowledge, skills, or abilities. The scope of the microcredential can be as granular as a single skill or competency."

A microcredential can take different forms, allowing your organization some creativity and flexibility in how you use this option. As the name suggests, the scope of the microcredential is narrower than a certification. However, the narrower scope does not imply the microcredential is less valuable to the target audience.

Microcredentials can be used in a variety of ways within a portfolio of credentialing products. Microcredentials are valuable to create an entry path to the profession, support ongoing professional development with new skills, or complement existing credentials to recognize achievement in advanced areas. They can also be stacked to signal a broader achievement.

For example, a series of ABC programs may result in microcredentials that can be stacked to earn a certificate. Another option is to award a microcredential related to an advanced skill or topic that can be added onto an existing certification.

Regardless of how they are used, carefully consider the development of the microcredential and utilize similar approaches as discussed earlier in this section to build them.

Section 3: GROW

Chapter 8
Maintain Momentum

LAUNCHING A NEW credentialing program is a tremendous accomplishment. Managing and growing the program requires the same amount of care, attention to detail, and careful planning that you applied during program design and launch.

Ongoing Tasks

Whether your organization has a certification program, an assessment-based certificate program, or both, you have an obligation to credential holders, employers, and the public to maintain those programs. Credentials that are current, accurate, and relevant are better positioned to retain value to program stakeholders.

The typical activities associated with ongoing management are listed in the table below for both ABC and certification programs. Planning and budgeting for these activities are essential for success.

Assessment-Based Certificate (ABC) Programs	Certification Programs
Evaluation of training content	Analysis of exam performance
Evaluation of instructors and/or training delivery	Evaluation of eligibility and recertification requirements
Recruiting and training SMEs	Recruiting and training SMEs
Data-driven training content and assessment review and updates	Ongoing exam development activities
Maintain a pipeline of qualified instructors	Maintain a pipeline of qualified candidates for the governing board and committee positions

For ABC programs, keeping the training content up to date and accurate includes gathering feedback from course instructors and participants, monitoring content as changes occur over time, and conducting periodic Needs Analysis and/or Job Analysis studies, to gather additional data to support content changes. Of course, as changes to the course are made, corresponding updates must also be made to the assessment.

For certifiction programs, ongoing exam development is required. Several factors drive the frequency of exam-development activities, including the pace of change in the role being certified, volume of test takers, security considerations, and other factors.

A typical process to conduct ongoing exam development is outlined below. The specific frequency of these activities, along with the steps involved, are best planned and designed in close consultation with a psychometrician and other measurement professionals, as needed.

Job Analysis: Typically conducted every five years, the Job Analysis informs any changes to the exam content outline and test specifications. After each Job Analysis, the following activities typically occur:

Exam content outline: The domains, domain weights, and tasks are updated.

Item reclassification: Items are re-coded to the new content outline.

Item and test-form development: New exam form(s) built to meet the updated test specifications.

Standard Setting: A cut-score study is conducted to establish the passing point for the base form of the exam.

Ongoing item development: Item writing, item review, and test form development typically occur on an annual basis, with new forms being released and older test forms being retired. The psychometrician plays a key role as new forms are developed to ensure they are equivalent in content and difficulty to the base form.

Ongoing exam evaluation: Monitor item and test performance regularly to identify issues and correct problems.

An organization administering a certification program also has an obligation to the program stakeholders to implement exam administration procedures fairly and consistently. Making exceptions to a policy is generally not a good practice, because it can penalize a participant or give them an unfair advantage.

Performance Monitoring

A monitoring system collects feedback and data to measure program performance and informs the quality-management system discussed later in this chapter. Your organization can define the activities used to monitor performance.

They should generally include analyzing exam/assessment data, evaluating vendor performance and deliverables, overseeing exam delivery activities, watching financial performance, conducting staff member evaluations, implementing a process for board and committee self-evaluation, and gathering feedback from applicants, certificate holders, and/or certificants.

Marketing and Communications

Clear and frequent communications with the target audience and other key stakeholders should begin during the initial development of the program and continue throughout. Develop a robust marketing strategy, identify clear key messages, and ensure all staff members and volunteer leaders work together to implement the plan.

The value of the program may be different for each stakeholder. It is important to work with an experienced professional to customize the message and approach for each audience.

Relationship Management

No program successfully operates in a vacuum. Maintaining positive relationships with stakeholders has many benefits and provides a strong foundation for continual program growth and improvement.

Retaining high-performing staff members, consultants, and vendors in key positions builds a depth of program understanding and preserves historical knowledge.

Building an engaged community of certificants, who see value in the organization and credential, results in a pool of ambassadors to promote the program.

Engaging a diverse group of thought leaders, SMEs, and stakeholders provides new ideas and perspectives to your organization and program(s).

Communicating clearly and frequently with related membership organizations, any parent organization, and/or other key stakeholder groups builds trust and understanding.

Most credentialing programs depend heavily on networks of volunteer leaders and members of the profession to maintain the program. Recruiting leaders and content experts is challenging but vital to the success of the program. It is also required to align with best practices and third-party accreditation standards.

You should plan early on for how you will recruit volunteer leaders and SMEs in order to maintain a healthy pipeline and avoid overdependence on a few key contributors. Building low-barrier pathways to becoming involved, using term limits, and providing recognition for SME contributions, will aid in continually bringing in new ideas and perspectives to keep the program relevant.

Intellectual Property Protection

The content you have developed is among the most valuable assets of the program and, possibly, the organization. Programs must carefully guard training and exam content.

Intellectual property (IP) protection includes rigorous security procedures throughout the development and delivery phases, consistent use and enforcement of confidentiality and conflict of interest agreements, filing for copyright and trademark protections, and clearly addressing intellectual property ownership and use in agreements with SMEs.

Chapter 9
Continual Improvement

Quality Management

Policies and procedures provide the framework for delivering a fair and valuable credentialing program. Adding a quality-management system and process ensures that policies and procedures are implemented as intended. It also provides a mechanism for identifying problems and helps staff look beyond day-to-day management activities to make systemic improvements.

A variety of factors promote an organizational culture that values continuous improvement through a well-defined quality-management system, including the following:

- Defining a clear connection between quality and the program's vision and strategic goals keeps it as a relevant and timely topic.
- Committing to quality management through the allocation of resources increases success. Resources

include creating a dedicated quality-manager role, developing tools to manage the system, and providing training throughout the organization.

- Correcting errors and preventing issues while actively looking for ways to improve effectiveness and efficiency.
- Demonstrating the value of the quality-management system by celebrating successes and highlighting improvements.

The quality-management process should include the following components:

- Quality-management policies that define the requirements of the management system and establish a quality-manager role.
- Internal quality audit to confirm that policies are being implemented as written, needed changes are identified, and problems are addressed.
- Management review to ensure root-cause analyses are conducted, preventative and corrective actions are identified and assigned, and that resources are allocated as needed.
- Logging to track and evaluate activities.
- Documentation management procedures (e.g., version control, naming conventions, document control) to ensure that current, approved versions of policies, SOPs, forms, and other items are readily available.

Threat Analysis

Each program faces a unique set of challenges, or threats, that require customized mitigation planning. Threats evolve over time and vary based on industry, organization type, size, and other factors. A threat analysis allows each organization to describe, evaluate, and strategize for its unique set of circumstances.

Organizations conduct a threat analysis to accomplish two goals:
1. Identify risks to the ability to make decisions, operate impartially, and carry out the organization's purpose; and
2. To develop plans or identify strategies to mitigate the potential damage from the identified risks.

A threat analysis formally describes the threats to all, or parts, of the program and identifies ways to minimize those threats. Threats may be actual, potential, or perceived risks and/or vulnerabilities that could negatively impact the organization or credentialing program. By identifying risks, understanding potential effects, and strategizing to minimize or mitigate negative impacts, programs shift from a reactive to proactive mode.

Using a threat analysis to identify the severity and likelihood of risks allows for prioritized planning by focusing on the risks most likely to cause significant harm. The threat-analysis process contributes to the quality-management system and supports required security planning, impartial governance, and policy implementation.

Each threat analysis builds on the previous analysis as new challenges are identified and the effectiveness of previous planning is evaluated and adjusted. The threat-analysis plan should be updated annually and anytime a significant change occurs in the business environment, governance structure, or program operations.

Third-Party Accreditation

The audit and management review components of the quality-management system described earlier in this chapter provide an internal system to ensure policies and procedures are followed. Many programs benefit from the added rigor of third-party accreditation from an outside, objective entity.

I.C.E. defines accreditation as, "the process by which an agency having authority grants time-limited formal recognition to an institution, organization, business, credentialing body, or other independent entity, after verifying that the aforementioned has met predetermined and standardized criteria."[1]

Accreditation confirms the program meets a predetermined set of standards and holds the program accountable for continuing compliance with those standards through a peer-review system. Credentialing programs often report that obtaining accreditation increases credibility, builds legal defensibility, provides a competitive advantage, ensures better consistency and fairness, and improves processes.

---

[1] I.C.E. Terminology Task Force, (2020). *Basic Guide to Credentialing Terminology (2nd ed.)*. Institute for Credentialing Excellence.

NAVIGATING CREDENTIALS

In the United States, the following standards are widely recognized for ABC programs and certification programs in any field of practice.

Standard	Accrediting Body
ABC Programs	
ICE 1100:2019 – Standard for Assessment-Based Certificate Program	Institute for Credentialling Excellence (I.C.E.) Assessment-based Certificate Accreditation Council (ACAC)
ASTM E2659-18 Standard Practice for Certificate Programs	ANSI National Accreditation Board (ANAB)
Certification Programs	
National Commission for Certifying Agencies (NCCA) Standards for the Accreditation of Certification Programs	NCCA (a division of I.C.E.)
ISO/IEC 17024 Conformity assessment – General requirements for bodies operating certification of persons	ANSI National Accreditation Board (ANAB)

Seeking accreditation includes first selecting an accreditation standard. While there is considerable overlap across the standards, each has benefits and requirements that may better suit a particular program.

Once a standard has been selected, conduct an analysis to determine gaps in compliance and corrective actions. A gap analysis provides a detailed picture of the time, tasks, and resources needed to bring the program into full accreditation compliance.

Building a project plan with this information will guide the next phase of accreditation preparation. The application process begins once the program is reasonably certain that all the accreditation standards are met.

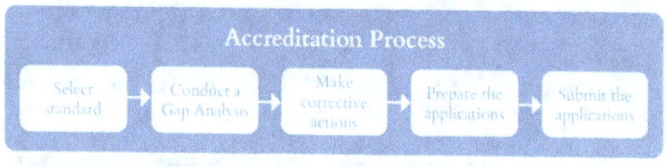

Each accrediting body has its own application-review process that results in an accreditation decision. Accreditation is typically granted for a five-year period with annual reporting requirements.

Chapter 10

Planning for Growth

YOUR PROGRAM GROWS through a continual process of analyzing and adapting to meet the changing needs of the primary stakeholders. Organizations evaluate and update policies, review training content for relevancy, release new exam forms, identify and implement improvements, and much more. Without these activities, the program would quickly become outdated and lose value.

Effective planning, both short- and long-term, serves as the foundation of a successful program. Planning helps your organization accomplish its mission, increase its impact, and address priorities with intention and focus.

You should plan an interactive process involving both staff and volunteer leadership, in order to evaluate the current environment, identify strengths, challenges, opportunities, and threats, discuss trends, and set strategic goals and objectives.

References and Resources

Accreditation Standards

ASTM E2659-18 Standard Practice for Certificate Programs

ICE 1100: 2019 – Standard for Assessment-Based Programs

ISO/IEC 17024 - Conformity assessment — General requirements for bodies operating certification of persons (2012)

National Commission for Certifying Agencies Standards for the Accreditation of Certification Programs (2021)

Publications

Certification: The I.C.E. Handbook, 3rd Edition. Institute for Credentialing Excellence (2019).

Certification & Accreditation Law Handbook, 3rd Edition. American Society of Association Executives (2016).

Basic Guide to Credentialing Terminology (2nd ed.). I.C.E. Terminology Task Force, Institute for Credentialing Excellence (2020).

Defining Features of Quality Certification and Assessment-Based Certificate Programs. Institute for Credentialing Excellence (2010).

To Validity and Beyond! A Handbook for Credentialing Exams. Dainis, Amanda (2021).

Industry Associations

Institute for Credentialing Excellence (I.C.E.) (www.credentialingexcellence.org)

Association of Test Publishers (ATP) (www.testpublishers.org/)

American Society of Association Executives (ASAE) (www.asaecenter.org/)

SeaCrest Toolkits

The following toolkits are available from the SeaCrest website at www.seacrestcompany.com/teachable-toolkits/:

- Certification Governing Body: An Onboarding Kit
- Quality Management Systems
- Creating Successful RFPs for Certification Programs
- Threat Analysis

Acknowledgments

THANK YOU TO Ashley Bardsley, Erin Deist, and Lisa Seyfried. We appreciate the trust you put in us and are thankful for your creative contributions and commitment to the SeaCrest team.

We wrote this book based on our combined experiences working with certification and certificate programs. What we learned over the years directly results from the generosity of the many colleagues, clients, and consultants who have shared their experiences and expertise with us. Their insights and collaboration are invaluable. We are grateful to be part of the community of credentialing professionals who generously share their time, knowledge, and expertise to make credentials work better for everyone.

To Wade Delk, Leon Gross, Shannon Carter, and Amin Sair, we owe our profound gratitude for your unwavering support and encouragement. We also extend deep thanks to our many colleagues and friends in the credentialing community, too many to list, who have helped us learn and grow through the years.

We are thankful for the associations that bring our credentialing community together, providing space for learning, networking, and collaborating. The Institute for

NAVIGATING CREDENTIALS

Credentialing Excellence, the Association of Test Publishers (ATP), the Certification Networking Group (CNG), and the American Board of Nursing Specialties (ABNS) provide invaluable support and community for the volunteers who lend their time to advance our profession.

Together with those associations are the accrediting bodies that apply the standards for quality credentials: the ANSI National Accreditation Board (ANAB), the Accreditation Board for Specialty Nursing Certification (ABSNC), and the National Commission for Certifying Agencies (NCCA). The staff and volunteers who support these organizations are central to the success of the certification community.

Our deepest gratitude goes to our families, who have been patient, understanding, and relentlessly supportive as we balance our time between professional and family commitments.

About the Authors

JANICE MOORE AND CYNTHIA ALLEN co-founded SeaCrest Consulting in 2006 to serve as a resource for organizations seeking to build, improve, and grow certification programs. Together, the SeaCrest team brings decades of experience developing credentials and helping organizations meet best practices. They share a deep understanding of the application and interpretation of accreditation standards and the workings of the NCCA, ANAB, and ABSNC accrediting processes, as evidenced in the more than 400 successful accreditation applications submitted by SeaCrest.

Janice Moore, ICE-CCP

Leveraging twenty-five years of experience in the certification industry, including her previous role with the Institute of Credentialing Excellence (I.C.E.) and the National Commission for Certifying Agencies (NCCA), Janice serves as a strategic partner for organizations seeking to develop new credentials, improve existing programs, and achieve accreditation.

After working with clients across dozens of industries to develop their certification programs, Janice firmly believes that accreditation standards are an effective framework for improvement. Janice serves as a strategic-planning partner to evaluate and improve clients' major program areas, helping to set goals, assess feasibility, develop strong governance foundations, facilitate policy development, and design quality-management programs.

In addition to volunteering throughout her community, Janice remains committed to the certification industry through a number of volunteer activities. She often presents at industry conferences, has participated on numerous I.C.E. committees, and served on the I.C.E. Board of Directors, I.C.E. Accreditation Services Council, I.C.E. Certification Services Council, and ANSI National Accreditation Board (ANAB) Personnel Certification Accreditation Committee (PCAC).

Janice's love for animals is evident in her hobbies and volunteerism. When she's not working with her dogs, she can often be found educating guests about birds of prey and wildlife conservation on the trails of the Carolina Raptor Center.

Cynthia Allen, ICE-CCP

Utilizing more than twenty years of experience in certification-program development and maintenance, accreditation, project management, and marketing-communications, Cynthia provides strategic guidance to organizations seeking to improve their programs and their stakeholder communications. She supports SeaCrest's overall belief that certification programs, no matter the size or scope, can make a positive impact.

Cynthia's focus at SeaCrest is to build relationships with clients, serve as a strategic partner to volunteer and staff leaders, and provide experienced project management. As an active member of the credentialing community, she believes in sharing knowledge and experience to build a stronger and connected credentialing community.

Cynthia is a longtime member and volunteer of I.C.E. She served on the Board of Directors of the Certification Network Group (CNG) and has shared her experience through speaking engagements at conferences and webinars hosted by I.C.E, the American Board of Nursing Specialties (ABNS), and the American Society of Association Executives (ASAE).

Cynthia studied marketing and communications at Virginia Tech and earned a master's degree in journalism at New York University. She is a fierce fan of the Virginia Tech Hokies and enjoys spending time with her husband and two children (also loyal Hokies fans).

While she may live inside the Capital Beltway, collaboration and teamwork with clients and staff are essential to her working style and to delivering top-notch results.

Ashley Bardsley, ICE-CCP

Ashley has twenty years of experience in customer service, operations analysis, project management, quality improvement, policy development, and accreditation compliance and has supported credentialing organizations for the past twelve years in her roles with SeaCrest.

Ashley's previous experience includes working as a business analyst for Coach, Inc., where she facilitated process improvements within the business units, developed reporting tools and analysis, and created forecast planning models; and working with Jockey, International as a liaison between company-owned facilities and domestic and international contractors, to ensure supply-chain integrity and efficient process flow.

Ashley holds a BS in Textile and Apparel Management from North Carolina State University and has completed the I.C.E. Credentialing Specialist Certificate program. She earned the I.C.E Certified Credentialing Professional (ICE-CCP) in 2021. Lucky enough to live in a coastal town, Ashley loves salt air and salt water and spends as much time as she can enjoying both with her husband and two children.

Lisa Seyfried, ICE-CCP

Lisa Seyfried serves as the Manager, Accreditation and Credentialing Services for SeaCrest. In this role, Lisa partners with credentialing organizations to evaluate programs, find areas for improvement, and achieve third-party accreditation. Prior to this role, she was the Quality Manager for the Human Resource Certification Institute (HRCI), where she managed the accreditation of HRCI's exams, oversaw the quality-management system, and implemented process improvements for the certification programs. Lisa has nearly a decade of experience applying both NCCA and IEC/ISO 17024 standards, auditing certification programs for compliance, implementing process improvements, and managing quality management systems.

Lisa earned a Bachelor of Science in Psychology from Jefferson University, and a Master of Arts in Industrial/Organizational Psychology from the Chicago School of Professional Psychology. In her free time, Lisa enjoys crocheting and chasing after her two kids.

Erin Deist

Erin Deist joined the SeaCrest team as the Manager, Credentialing Services in 2024. With a substantial background in customer service, she applies a customer-first focus to this position. Prior to working at SeaCrest, Erin worked for the Behavior Analyst Certification Board (BACB) as a Certification Program Coordinator for their BCBA and BCaBA programs.

Erin earned a Bachelor of Science in Hospitality and Tourism from Southern Illinois University Carbondale. Living in the suburbs of Chicago, Erin enjoys spending her free time exploring the city, hanging out with her nieces and nephew, and spoiling her dog, Leroy.

www.ingramcontent.com/pod-product-compliance
Lightning Source LLC
Chambersburg PA
CBHW071838210526
45479CB00001B/189